The Seal on the Rocks

Text by Doug Allan

**Photographs by
Oxford Scientific Films**

Methuen Children's Books
in association with Belitha Press

Contents

Note : The use of a capital letter for a seal's name indicates that it is a specific *type* (or species) of seal (ie Northern Elephant Seal) and the use of lower case means that it is a member of a larger *group* of seals.

Grey Seals rest on the seaweed-covered rocks at low tide.

Grey Seals poke their heads up out of the sea to look at what's happening onshore.

Where seals live

Seals are *mammals* that spend much of their lives in water. Like other mammals, they are warmblooded (which means that their bodies stay at a constant temperature even on cool days or in cold water) and covered with hair. Seals have lungs, so although they often dive under water, they must return to the surface to breathe. The females give birth to live young, which they feed with milk produced in their own bodies.

Millions of years ago, the ancestors of seals lived completely on land. Seals' skeletons and limbs show that they were once able to walk on all fours, but their legs have since *evolved* into *flippers* for swimming, and their bodies have become smooth and streamlined, the best shape for diving.

Seals are well adapted for spending long periods in the water, completely at ease through the roughest storms, catching all their food beneath the waves. Some *species,* like the Harp Seals, make long journeys as they follow the shoals of fish and shrimps that they feed on. Other kinds, like the Grey Seals off the British coast, keep to one stretch of shoreline when they are adults. Here, they learn all the best fishing places, and don't wander far.

But seals are never completely aquatic, they still like to get out onto the rocks or onto a beach, where they can lie in the wind and sun for long periods, resting and sleeping. They also have to come ashore to give birth to their young, although there are some kinds of seal pups which can swim almost as soon as they are born.

On shore, seals don't have the same grace and agility that they show in the water. They have to drag their heavy bodies around in a clumsy fashion because their flippers just aren't designed for movement on land. Where there are land *predators,* the seals are always wary, ready to go back into the water if danger threatens.

Seals, therefore, spend their lives in two very different types of *habitat*. Some of the time they are in the water, but they also come on shore. We shall see how well they manage to survive in both places.

The Pacific Monk Seal lives on beaches in Hawaii.

Seals around the world

Seals live in many different places around the world. Monk Seals are found in the warm waters of the Mediterranean and on some of the Hawaiian Islands in the Pacific. One of the largest seals, the Northern Elephant Seal, lives off the coasts of Mexico and California. A male can be 14 ft (3.5 m) long from its nose to the tips of its rear flippers, and may weigh up to 2.5 tons (2.5 tonnes). That's as much as two motor cars! There is one kind of seal which lives only in fresh water, the Baikal Seal which is found in the landlocked Lake Baikal in Russia.

Most seals, however, inhabit the *temperate* and polar regions of the world. Here, both the weather and the seas are fairly cool, there is an abundance of food and they are less disturbed by humans. The commonest seal in the world is the Crabeater. It lives in the Antarctic and has a population of about 30 million.

Most types of seals are solitary creatures when they are at sea. Fish shoals concentrated in one area may cause a number of seals to gather at that place, but usually they search for food independently.

Right : Northern Elephant Seals love to lie together. It helps them to stay warm, and sometimes they roar and jostle with each other for the most comfortable position!

Harbour Seals are fairly common on coastlines all round the north Atlantic and the north Pacific Oceans.

When they do come ashore, seals never venture far from water simply because it is so much effort for them to move on land. The Common Seals found around Britain prefer to rest in *estuaries* and bays. As the tide falls, they settle on banks of sand and mud, or on seaweed-covered rocks, where they can rest safely, basking in the sun until the tide returns. Grey Seals, which live on both sides of the North Atlantic, haul themselves out on remote rocky islands and parts of the coast which are steep or fairly difficult for humans to reach.

Southern Elephant Seals don't seem to mind sharing their beach with penguins.

Crabeater Seals spend all their lives among the freezing ice floes of Antarctica.

In the polar regions, the beaches and rocks are often covered with snow and ice. The sea itself may be partly frozen so that there are many *floes*. Some seals may spend their entire lives without truly coming ashore, pulling themselves out instead onto this floating sea-ice. They may stay well scattered among the floes throughout the year. Other kinds of seals, however, congregate in colonies, especially during the breeding season. In some places, hundreds of females (called 'cows') gather with smaller numbers of males (called 'bulls') on the same beach.

The Hooded Seal from the Arctic can inflate its nose so it looks like a red balloon. It does this when it is angry or frightened.

You can see the five claws quite clearly on the front flipper of this Common Seal.

The seal's body

Although they spend some of their time hauled out on rocks, sandy beaches or even on snow and ice, seals are really much better adapted for living in water than on land. Their sleek streamlined shape, the head merging into the body with no obvious neck, lets them move through the water with only the smallest effort. For swimming, seals have flippers – a pair near the front of the body and a pair right at the rear. These flippers are actually modified arms and legs, in which the long bones have become very shortened, while the fingers and toes have lengthened. Skin has developed as webbing between the individual fingers and toes, giving the seal its four broad, paddle-like flippers. If you look closely at a flipper, you will still see the five claws near the edge, the animal's equivalent of your finger or toe nails.

The broad, webbed hind flippers of the Southern Elephant Seal make it a powerful swimmer in the water.

Because seals are warmblooded animals, the temperature of their bodies stays quite high even when they are swimming in cold water. The dense covering of fine hairs over their bodies stops them losing some heat, but the layer of fatty *blubber* under their skin is much more important in keeping them warm. Imagine that your rubber boots were your skin, then your socks would be like the seal's blubber. Some species of seal have a thicker blubber layer in winter, when the sea is colder, than in summer – just as you wear extra heavy socks in chilly weather!

The blubber is also important in two other ways. First, it helps the seals to stay afloat while out at sea. Then, when they come ashore and sometimes have to haul themselves over rough ground, the blubber layer acts like a cushion. It prevents injury and makes it more comfortable for the seals to lie out on the rocks.

Seals vary a lot in their colouring, although they are usually shades of brown or grey. Some, like the Grey Seal, are dappled or spotted. Others, like the Elephant Seal, are all one colour. But most seals are paler on the underside of their bodies than on the upper surfaces. This is a form of *camouflage*, which makes it harder for them to be seen by the fish they are hunting in the sea.

The mottled grey and white colouring of these Grey Seals is good camouflage as they lie on the rocks.

This male Southern Elephant Seal is roaring out a challenge to other males during the breeding season.

The seal's head

Seals have handsome, alert faces and they look a bit like dogs. Their nostrils are right at the tip of the nose, in the best place for easy breathing in a rough sea. They have a good sense of smell, which they don't use underwater when their nostrils are closed, but need on land for recognizing their own pups on the often crowded beaches where the seals breed.

The male Elephant Seal has an extra purpose for his big nose. During the mating season, the males snort air into their noses to puff them out and so increase the volume of their roaring.

A seal's long whiskers grow out from its cheeks. These are very sensitive to touch, and with them, seals may be able to detect movement in the water caused by fish or other animals they are hunting.

Their big round eyes are good for seeing in the dim underwater light where they catch their food. They are reckoned to see as well in the water as a cat does on land. Having both eyes pointing forward means that seals can accurately judge distance, which is very important when they are chasing fast-moving *prey*. To protect the surface of their eyes, but at the same time allow them to be kept open, seals have a transparent *membrane*, like a second eyelid, which they can pull across in front of their eyes. When

The big eyes and long whiskers of this Southern Elephant Seal help it to hunt for fish in the darkness of the deep ocean.

Elephant Seals lie on the beach, they often have sand flipped in their faces by neighbours lumbering past, but they clean their eyes by flicking this membrane across, like the windscreen wipers on a car.

Although they do not have the fleshy outer flap that we call an ear (it has disappeared to make their bodies even more streamlined for swimming), seals still have an acute sense of hearing both underwater and on land. The two openings to the inner ear mechanisms are tiny holes hidden under the hair on the head. Seals use hearing to seek their prey, to find their pups on the beach, and to communicate with other seals in the water. They make a variety of sounds while swimming beneath the surface – clicks, whistles and grunts – but scientists still have to find out exactly what message is meant by each.

Seals don't have visible ear flaps like we have, but they still possess an acute sense of hearing.

When they are swimming slowly, seals use their front flippers in a 'dog-paddle' style. This is a Common Seal.

Seal movement in water

A seal is perfectly at home in the water, floating at the surface, diving beneath, gliding along at any angle, often on one side, or even upside down. When it is swimming fast, it holds its front flippers pressed tightly against its body, making its shape as streamlined as possible. All the power comes from the movement of the rear half of its body and its hind flippers.

During its stroke to one side, each hind flipper is spread wide, like the tail of a fish, then it is folded and made narrow as it is pulled back across. So the flippers open and close alternately, while the seal is also swinging the rear part of its body from side to side, using the strong muscles in its flexible spine. The seal steers using its front flippers. When the animal wants to change direction quickly, say to the left, it arches its back in that direction then puts out its right front flipper, using it as a paddle to give itself a push round.

A young Southern Elephant Seal rests in shallow water.

Seals can swim in short bursts at a speed of up to 15 mph (23 kph), either chasing their own prey or escaping from danger themselves. But usually, seals cruise more slowly, at about 5 mph (8 kph) underwater, so their oxygen lasts longer. They always have to return to the surface for air, but some can hold their breath and stay underwater for a remarkably long time. The champion diver so far measured is the Northern Elephant Seal, which can remain submerged for an hour and reach a depth of 2,350 ft (700 m). As soon as it dives, the seal diverts its blood flow away from parts of its body which are not directly involved with swimming. This means that it uses less oxygen and can stay underwater for a greater length of time.

When a seal is at sea, it can sleep by floating vertically at the surface with its nose stuck into the air, so that it looks like a floating bottle bobbing in the waves. It can also lie horizontally, with only its back breaking the water and its head underneath, coming up for a few breaths every time it needs more oxygen.

You can see how the Crabeater Seal in the middle of the group is using its front flippers for turning in the water.

Seal movement on land

While in the sea, a seal is effectively weightless, being just the right buoyancy for swimming. But if you watch a seal, especially a big heavy one, pull itself through the breaking surf and up the shore, it is obvious that this is hard work for the animal. It has to drag its full weight around, and its body is simply not the best shape for this. Because of the effort involved, a seal never really goes further from the water than is necessary.

To move on land, the seal uses a 'humping' action. It first presses its foreflippers forward and down against the ground. Then the seal lifts its head and front part of its body and levers itself forward, at the same time arching its back so that the rear quarters are pulled along.

The Grey Seal can make a 'hook' grip with its foreflippers.

The foreflipper skeleton is similar to your hand and arm.

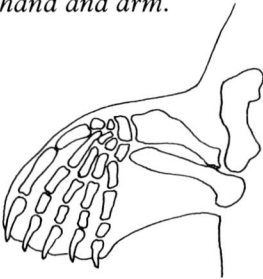

1. The front flippers are placed forward . . .

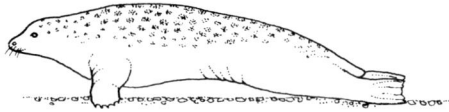

2. . . . then the seal raises itself on them.

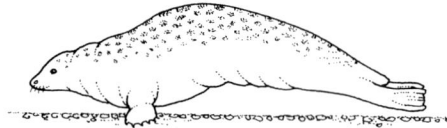

3. It arches its back.

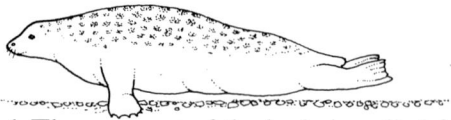

4. The rear part of the body is pulled forward.

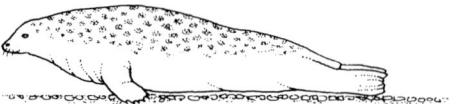

Seal movement

5. The seal is then ready to go through the action again.

Some kinds of seals, like this young Grey Seal, can curl the tips of their flippers over to gain a hook-like grip on the rocks as they move.

This movement is very slow and clumsy going uphill, but on a downhill stretch the heavy body can hump along quite quickly. When alarmed, a seal fairly bounces towards the sea over a smooth slope such as sand, pebbles or snow – faster than a man can run. You can actually see daylight between the body and the ground at each violent bounce.

Seals which normally live in the polar regions have a slightly easier job. By swimming fast underwater, they can shoot up out from the sea straight onto the ice floes. Crabeater Seals make their way across the snow by a sort of slithering movement, vigorously thrashing their hind quarters from side to side, while pulling themselves along with alternate backward strokes of their front flippers.

Crabeater Seals can move over ice floes at up to 15 mph (23 kph).

Food and feeding

All seals are *carnivorous*. Some kinds eat a wide range of food, while others have more specialized diets. Common Seals and Grey Seals catch squid (an animal like an octopus), shrimps and many types of fish such as sea trout, salmon, cod, flatfishes and eels. Sometimes they hunt near the shore, peering into rock crevices and pushing aside the seaweed fronds, then darting after any fish or other animals. The eels they catch may be as long as the seals themselves. They bring them to the surface, holding them in their front flippers while the eels wriggle furiously. The seals then bite away and swallow chunks of the flesh along the body of the eel from head to tail, rather like you eat corn-on-the-cob. They may leave the tough head and backbone uneaten.

When they hunt in the open sea, over deep water, seals often dive down below the shoals of fish or squid. Looking upwards, they are more easily able to see their prey silhouetted against the available surface light. However, good eyesight does not seem to be essential for them to catch their food, because totally blind yet healthy seals have been found in many places. Their acute hearing and their sensitive whiskers, which can detect movement, must also be very important in helping them to find their prey.

The Leopard Seal eats penguins, and has extra large front flippers so it can turn fast in pursuit of them.

Crabeater Seals swim just below the sea ice in search of their food, krill.

Crabeater Seals that live around Antarctica eat only *krill*, small shrimp-like *crustaceans* that exist in huge shoals. The Crabeater Seal has teeth at the back of its upper and lower jaws which are specially modified to enable it to catch the krill more efficiently. The seal feeds by swimming into a shoal of krill with its mouth open, sucking them in and sieving them from the water using the arrangement of teeth like a strainer. It then lifts its tongue into the roof of its mouth, pushing out the water between the teeth, but keeping back the krill for swallowing.

Seals can extract all the water they need from the food they eat, so they don't have to drink while at sea.

You can see how, in the skull of this Crabeater Seal, the teeth mesh together to sieve the krill from the water.

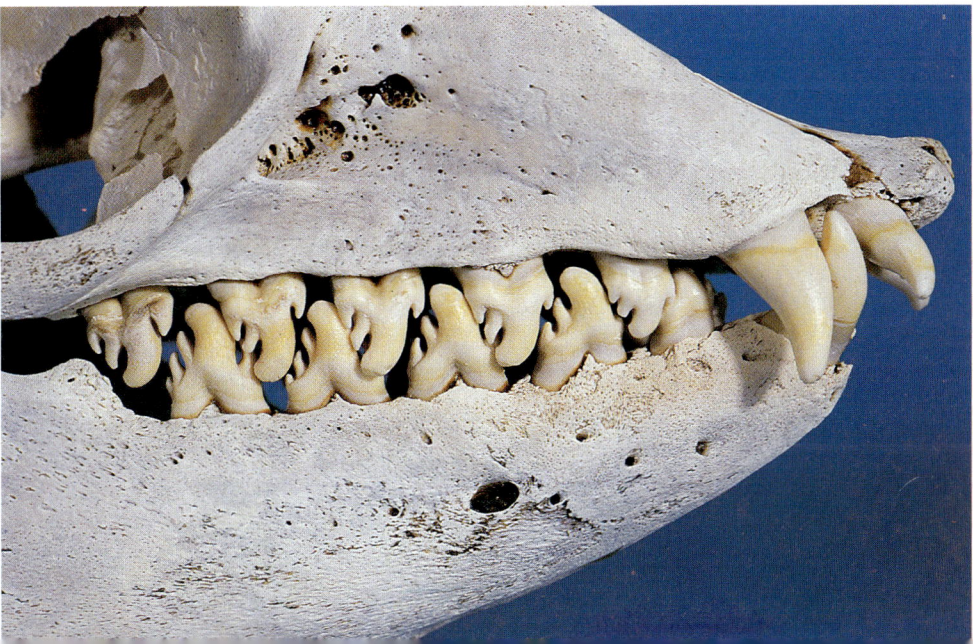

Southern Elephant Seals stay cool on warm days by flicking wet gravel onto their backs.

Coping with heat and cold

With their layers of blubber, seals are better able to withstand cold conditions in the water than warm weather on land. They frequently have problems with overheating, so when they are lying ashore on sunny, mild days, seals do various things which help them to stay cool.

They use their flippers, which don't have much blubber, like radiators, pumping a lot of blood around them to carry heat away from their bodies. If there is a slight wind, they hold their flippers up to be cooled even more. Elephant Seals cool themselves down by using their front flippers to flick wet gravel from the beach up over their backs, or they make their way down to the sea where they are splashed by the waves. By these actions, they can stay cool and comfortable.

Every year, seals lose the old covering of hair over their bodies, and a new one grows in. This is called *moulting*. It takes about a month, and during this time, the seals stay on the rocks out of the water. For most types of seals, the old hair simply falls out and is replaced by new growth, but with Elephant Seals, the actual outer layer of their skin peels off as well.

Southern Elephant Seals like to lie in mud pools to soothe the irritation of their moulting.

It makes them look very tatty, and also seems to be very itchy and irritating for the animals. During their moult, Elephant Seals spend a lot of time scratching themselves with their flippers and lying in pools of mud, which makes them feel less uncomfortable.

Seals living in the icy polar regions of the world have an extra problem to cope with – each winter the sea freezes, yet they have to continue diving under the ice to find their food. Most roam about keeping in areas where the ice is broken up, for only there can they easily get in and out of the water. But Weddell Seals in Antarctica can stay in one place. They have specially angled front teeth, and by moving their head from side to side, they can saw and bite at the ice, thereby keeping holes in the ice open for breathing and hauling out. As the seals grow old, these teeth may become so old and diseased that the Weddells can't gnaw properly at the ice. They may be unable to get into the sea for food, or even be trapped under the ice and drown.

A female Weddell Seal enlarges her breathing hole by sawing at the edges with her teeth.

The birth of a Weddell Seal pup (above, middle and right). It emerges from the mother still inside the amniotic sac, but this soon bursts and the pup is lying on the snow, its eyes already open.

The breeding season

Young seals are called 'pups'. With most kinds of seals, the pups are born at the rookeries during the spring and summer, when the weather is kindest and there is most food available. But this is not always the case; the Grey Seals around Britain, for example, have their pupping season in the autumn and early winter.

The female seals haul out of the water shortly before they are ready to give birth. For seals of the temperate and tropical areas of the world, sheltered beaches and rocky shores are often the best places. For the polar seals, the ice floes of the frozen seas have to do. There may be males around too, but the females show no interest in them at this stage.

The actual birth of the pup is very quick, it usually takes only a minute or so. The amniotic sac (the thin bag of skin that surrounds the developing seal while it is still inside its mother) begins to be pushed out near the female's rear flippers. Sometimes it bursts as it comes out and the pup, still wet from the fluid that fills the sac, is delivered onto the ground. On other occasions, the sac will stay intact during the birth and only bursts when the pup moves its flippers. The mother rolls over to break the *umbilical cord,* then she sniffs at her newborn pup. It is by her own pup's individual smell that she will recognize it later when she returns from feeding trips.

With some species of seals, however, just before the females arrive to give birth, the males establish *territories*, areas of the beach which they claim as their own and which they defend against other males. The aggressive displays of the very largest seals, the Southern Elephant Seals, are particularly impressive. The two opponents bellow through their big inflated noses, then rear up and arch their backs. They slash at one another's necks with their teeth. The skin is very thick here, so usually no serious injuries occur, but fights can last for several hours until one seal is driven away.

Female seals usually gather within the territories of the males, and in this way, each male acquires a 'harem' – a collection of females with whom he may later mate – after they have given birth.

These two Southern Elephant Seals are fighting fiercely for territory on the breeding beach.

You can still see the stump of the umbilical cord attached to this young Weddell Seal pup, whose mother is using her body to shelter the pup from the blowing snow which covers her own body.

Rearing the young

Seals differ in the amount of protection they offer their young. Pups born to Grey Seals are not particularly fussed over by their mothers. Within a few hours of the birth, the parent goes to sea to feed, leaving the youngster on the beach. She returns four or five times in the first 24 hours to offer her baby milk, but after that, she normally visits it only twice a day, as the tide is coming in. The pup spends much of its time asleep, possibly pulling itself around a little, and crying out occasionally. When the mother comes back ashore, she is attracted to her own pup first by its bawling, then by its individual smell. If she is approached by a pup which is not her own, she may attack it quite savagely, tossing it aside with her teeth – and possibly injuring it. In those seal rookeries where there are many big bull seals, there is a danger that the pups may be killed by being crushed under these huge adults as they lumber around defending their territories.

Other kinds of seals, such as Common Seals or Weddell Seals, are much more protective mothers. They stay with their pups all the time for the first week or so, then coax them into the water for their introduction to swimming. If danger threatens, the Common Seal will hold her pup to her between her flippers while she swims away to escape.

Twin pups are extremely rare for the Weddell Seal, but this pair are doing well. One is suckling milk from its mother.

The seal feeds her pup with milk, which is white and creamy and thicker than cow's milk. The youngster nuzzles its mother in the region of her nipples until they become erect, then it *suckles*. The oily, slightly fishy tasting milk is very rich, and the pup rapidly puts on weight.

Depending on the species of seal, it takes from three weeks to two months before the pup is *weaned*. After this time, the mother leaves it to catch its own food and look after itself. By then, the youngster will have moulted the fine, often pale-coloured, coat of hair with which it was born and will look more like the adults in colour. After the pups are weaned, the females mate with the males, sometimes on land but quite often in the water. They become pregnant but will not give birth again until the following year.

This young Grey Seal is weaned and is moulting its baby coat of hair. It will wander far in the early years of its life, before settling down along one particular stretch of coastline.

Polar Bears feast on their seal kill.

Enemies and defence

Adult seals in temperate and tropical parts of the world are safe from natural predators on land (although, as we shall see, man is a very real enemy of some types of seal). Only in the frozen Arctic are they hunted on the ice floes by Polar Bears, who sometimes manage to creep up on sleeping seals and seize them with their sharp claws before they have a chance to escape into the water. The bears also crouch by the seals' breathing holes, waiting for them to return to the surface. When a seal comes up for air, the bear swings with its huge forepaw to lift the seal clean out of the water and onto the ice, where it is killed.

When they are being chased in the water, seals rely on their swimming speed to escape from predators. They can easily swim faster than Polar Bears, but some fall prey to Killer Whales and, in warmer waters, to sharks. Down in the Antarctic, Leopard Seals hunt young Crabeater Seals.

Young Crabeaters are born on the ice floes, and are protected by their mothers for the first weeks of their lives. But when they take to the water and have to look after themselves, then the danger from the Leopard Seals is greatest. Some Crabeaters are killed, but many also escape, judging by the large numbers of them that are seen with scars on their backs and flanks, caused by the attacks of Leopard Seals.

The Leopard Seal hunts young Crabeater Seals among the Antarctic ice floes.

Crabeater Seals are particularly inquisitive when they meet a scientific diver underwater.

Seals and people

Throughout history, in many parts of the world, people have hunted seals. In Britain, Grey Seals and Common Seals used to be killed for their skins, which were made into clothing and footwear. Oil was boiled out of the seals' flesh, and the blubber was stripped off to be burnt in special lamps for lighting and heat. In the last century, when large-scale catching of salmon began off the British coasts, fishermen found that seals, especially the Greys, were taking the fish too. The seals were raiding the fishing nets, cutting and damaging them with their sharp teeth and claws when they pulled out the salmon. The fishermen began shooting the seals. They killed so many that, about sixty years ago, it was realized that the numbers of seals had been reduced to a seriously low level. In 1932 a law was

By fixing numbered tags to the hind flippers of this Weddell Seal pup, scientists can check if it returns to its birthplace to breed in future years.

passed that prohibited the killing of seals at any time. This allowed the populations to build up again and, in 1970, the law was modified so that seals are now only completely protected during their breeding season, when they have pups. Fishermen who find seals round their nets, however, can still shoot them at any time.

In the Canadian Arctic, a great number of seal pups used to be hunted for their *pelts*. The hunters concentrated on the young seals because it was the pups which had the dense layer of fine hair, ideal for making coats. As recently as 1980, about 150,000 Harp Seal pups and 12,000 Hooded Seal pups were killed every year. For a long time, there had been two opposing views: people said that it was not right to kill the animals merely to provide fancy fur coats for rich people; on the other hand, the hunters claimed the seal populations were large enough for these thousands of pups to be removed without any danger at all to the overall balance of nature.

The arguments against the hunters finally won. Laws were passed in 1982 that prohibited the sale of seal pelts in Europe. When this last major market for the skins closed (they were already forbidden in the United States), the hunting stopped almost completely over the next three years. Now, a Canadian government investigation into the fur trade has recommended that there be an official ban on the seal killing, with no more licences to be issued.

Harp Seal pups are hunted for their white coats.

Hooker's Sea-lions are found to the south of New Zealand. With that shaggy 'mane' of hair around their necks, you will realize how they looked like 'lions of the sea' to people who first saw them.

Friends, neighbours and two close relatives

Many other animals live alongside seals on the shore and in the sea. On muddy beaches, gulls and wading birds strut amongst the basking seals, pecking at crabs and sea snails that they find in the mud. Down in Antarctica, penguins share floes with the seals, or waddle up past them on the shore on their way to their own breeding sites. In the rich oceans of both polar regions, whales and seals feed together on the huge shoals of shrimps.

Sea-lions and Walruses are two close relatives of the seals. In some parts of the world, they share habitats. Sea-lions and seals swim together in areas of the Pacific Ocean and Antarctica, while Walruses are found in the company of seals on beaches and ice floes in the Arctic.

This Southern Fur Seal is about to eat a fish. Can you see the little earflap on the side of the fur seal's head?

Sea-lions have sleek bodies and long flippers, quite similar to the so-called 'true' seals. But they are much more agile on land, because they are able to bend their hind flippers underneath their bodies so that their whole weight is supported on their four flippers. They can make their way across rocky ground much faster than the other seals. Also, if you look closely at a sea-lion's head, you will see two small flaps of skin which the true seals don't have, showing the position of the ears.

In the water, a sea-lion doesn't use its hind flippers for swimming, but trails them behind its body. It relies on beating its front flippers up and down for movement. It can swim quickly, and sometimes jumps clear of the water when travelling fast.

The sea-lions which live in the colder parts of the world's oceans have a thick covering of fine hairs next to their body, with coarser hair lying on top. They are called Fur Seals. Some kinds are still hunted by man for their pelts, although the numbers killed are strictly controlled.

The Walrus lives in the Arctic and is a big animal, over a ton (tonne) in weight, with unmistakeable long *tusks* curving down from its upper jaw. It has a rough and wrinkled skin, which looks too big for the animal inside.

Walruses love to lie together, and even with a whole beach to choose from, they crowd next to each other. The biggest bulls force their way to the middle of the group, jabbing at the others with their tusks until they reach the most comfortable position.

Walruses use their long tusks to rake up clams from the muddy seabed.
They suck out the flesh from the shells, or crush them between their front
flippers to get at the meat for eating.

Life on the rocks

Seals get energy for living and growing by feeding on various animals including fish, squid, shellfish and shrimps. In turn, seals themselves are eaten by animals such as sharks, Killer Whales and Polar Bears. These predators can also sometimes be *scavengers*, eating dead seals that they find. If a seal dies on the shore, gulls and crabs may be among the animals that dispose of the carcass. In this way, one animal becomes dependent on others for its survival. When we draw a diagram to represent such relationships, we call it a food chain.

Food chain

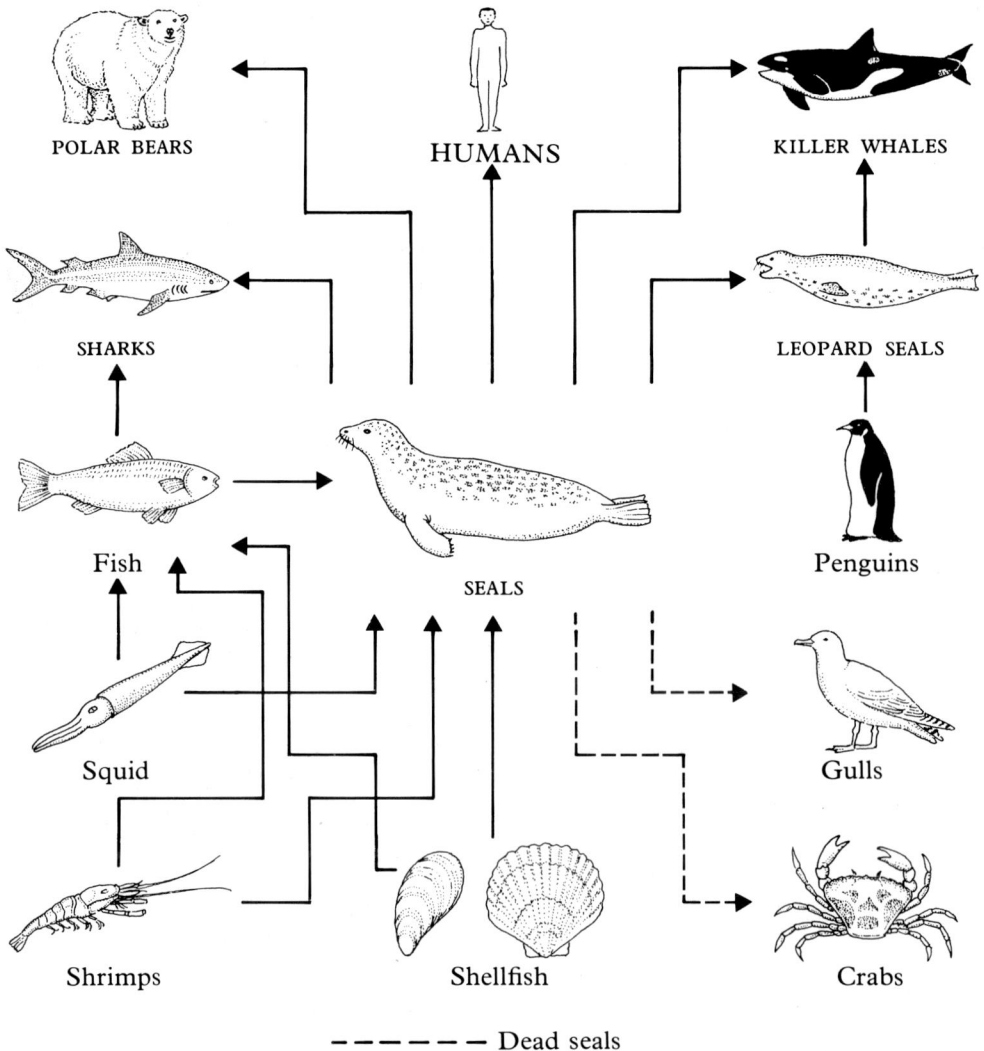

POLAR BEARS   HUMANS   KILLER WHALES

SHARKS   LEOPARD SEALS

Fish   SEALS   Penguins

Squid   Gulls

Shrimps   Shellfish   Crabs

– – – – – – Dead seals

This Grey Seal is about to go into the water.

Seals are beautifully adapted for life in the water, but they are also tied to the land for their breeding and moulting. It is while they are ashore that they are most threatened by the activities of humans, though the level of risk depends on exactly where in the world the seals live.

Fortunately today most kinds of seals are safe and flourishing, despite the hunting by salmon fishermen around Britain and elsewhere. But the position is not so good for Monk Seals, as their numbers are very low, particularly in the Mediterranean where *pollution* is a big problem. However, many people are actively helping towards the *conservation* of seals and their habitats. They are trying to protect stretches of the shore and even whole islands so that the seals can live there without interference. By creating these special nature reserves, people hope that the numbers of Monk Seals will increase and recover.

Seals keep to quiet places, and generally avoid busy beaches. You may see them in the sea, or occasionally ashore, if you make clifftop walks along remote parts of the coast. Next time you are on holiday at the seaside, look for special boat trips that go to the offshore islands where seals live. You will then have the best chance to see for yourself these fascinating and lovely animals as they bask on the rocks beside the sea.

Glossary

blubber : the layer of fat under a seal's skin **9, 18, 26**

camouflage : animal disguise – the way an animal hides itself by blending with its background so it cannot easily be seen **9**

carnivorous : meat-eating **16**

conservation : looking after animals and plants in their natural surroundings **31**

crustaceans : animals like shrimps or lobsters which have outer shells **17**

estuaries : the places where rivers run into the sea **6**

evolved : changed slowly over millions of years **3**

flippers : limbs modified for swimming – seals have four webbed, paddle-like flippers **3, 4, 8, 12, 13, 14, 15, 16, 18, 19, 21, 23, 28, 29**

floes : flat, floating pieces of ice **7, 15, 20, 24, 25, 28**

habitat : the natural home of any animal or plant **3, 28, 31**

krill : small shrimp-like crustaceans that are the food of Antarctic seals **17**

mammals : animals with hair or fur which feed their young on milk. Seals, dogs and humans are mammals **3**

membrane : a thin layer of skin **10, 11**

moulting : renewing the hair or fur on the body after shedding the old coat **19, 23, 31**

pelt : the skin and fur of an animal **27, 29, 31**

pollution : something which spoils or dirties the place where animals and plants live **31**

predator : an animal that hunts another animal for food **3, 24, 25, 30**

prey : an animal that is hunted and killed by another animal for food **10, 11, 13, 16, 25**

rookery : breeding site for seals **20, 22**

scavenger : an animal that feeds on the dead or dying remains of other animals **30**

species : a particular kind of animal or plant. A Crabeater is a species of seal **3, 9, 23**

suckle : (of young animals) to drink the mother's milk **23**

temperate : (of weather) neither very hot nor very cold **4, 20, 24**

territory : piece of land which an animal defends against intruders **21, 22**

tusks : enlarged front teeth of certain animals (ie Walrus, elephant) **29**

umbilical cord : the piece of skin that connects a female to her pup while the baby seal is still developing inside the mother's body **20, 22**

weaned : (of young animals) no longer dependent on their mother's milk for food, but able to eat other things **23**

First published in Great Britain 1988
by Methuen Children's Books Ltd
11 New Fetter Lane, London EC4P 4EE
Conceived, designed and produced by Belitha Press Ltd
31 Newington Green, London N16 9PU
Copyright © in this format Belitha Press Ltd 1988
Text © Oxford Scientific Films 1988
Series Editor: Jennifer Coldrey
Scientific Adviser: Dr Gwynne Vevers
Art Director: Treld Bicknell   Design: Naomi Games
ISBN 0 416 06512 0
Printed in Hong Kong by South China Printing Co.

The line drawings are by Lorna Turpin

The publishers wish to thank the following for permission to reproduce copyright material:
Doug Allan for pp. 6 *below*, 7 *above*, 8 *below*, 10, 12 *below*, 13, 17 *above*, 18, 19 *both*, 22, 23 *above*, 24 *below*, 25, 26 *above*, 28 *above* and front cover; pp. 20 *both* and 21 *above* (photographer Ken Richard); **Oxford Scientific Films Ltd.** for pp. 8 *above*, 12 *above* and title page (photographer Martyn Chillmaid); p. 2 and back cover (photographer Robin Redfern); pp. 3 and 23 *below* (photographer Tony Martin); p. 4 (photographer Maurice Tibbles); p. 5 (photographer E. R. Degginger); pp. 6 *above* and 29 (photographer Leonard Lee Rue III); pp. 7 *below*, 15 *below*, 21 *below*, 27 and 28 *below* (photographer T. S. McCann); p. 9 (photographer Jacki Sime); p. 11 *above* (photographer Michael Brooke); p. 11 *below* (photographer Tony Tilford); p. 15 *above* (photographer Peter O'Toole); p. 17 *below* (photographer C. J. Gilbert); p. 31 (photographers David and Sue Cayless); and Hugh Miles for the picture on p. 24.